DOCTOR WHO
· THE TARDIS INSIDE OUT ·
JOHN NATHAN-TURNER

DOCTOR WHO
·THE TARDIS INSIDE OUT·
JOHN NATHAN-TURNER
ILLUSTRATED BY ANDREW SKILLETER

By arrangement with the British Broadcasting Corporation

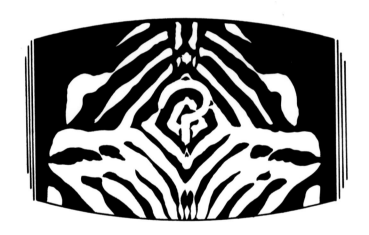

Random House 🏠 New York

CONTENTS

First American edition, 1985.
Originally published 1985 by Piccadilly Press Ltd., London,
England.
Second printing, 1986.
Published in the United States by Random House, Inc., New York,
and simultaneously in Canada by Random House of Canada Limited,
Toronto.

Library of Congress Cataloging in Publication Data: Nathan-Turner,
John, 1947– . Doctor Who : the Tardis inside out. SUMMARY:
Provides a behind-the-scenes look at the popular television
series and discusses the six actors who have portrayed Doctor
Who in the past twenty-one years. 1. Doctor Who (Television
program)—Juvenile literature. [1. Doctor Who (Television program)]
I. Skilleter, Andrew, ill.   II. Title.   PN1992.77.D6273N37
1985   791.45'72   85-2026   ISBN: 0-394-87415-3 (trade);
0-394-97415-8 (lib. bdg.)

Designed by Cherriwyn Magill
Manufactured in Belgium   2 3 4 5 6 7 8 9 0

The illustrations on pages 18, 19, 22, 23, 30, 31, 38, 39 are taken from poster prints by
Andrew Skilleter. They are available from: Who Dares Publishing,
c/o Lyle Stuart Inc., 120 Enterprise Avenue, Secaucus, N.J. 07094

William, Patrick, Jon, Tom, Peter and Colin. Six names that could be a list of friends, or enemies – add that magic ingredient "the Doctor", to the list, and all becomes clear. Six different actors who have played one of the most popular heroes of twentieth-century television – *Doctor Who* – that most British of British institutions.

All the actors who have played the part (and I am omitting Peter Cushing's movie performance, Trevor Martin's theater rôle, and the excellent masterpiece recreation of the first Doctor by the late Richard Hurndall in *The Five Doctors*), have acknowledged the fame the rôle brought them, and the magic associated with the show.

There have been nine producers of the "monster" product that is *Doctor Who*: Verity Lambert, John Wiles, Innes Lloyd, Peter Bryant, Derrick Sherwin, Barry Letts, Philip Hinchcliffe, Graham Williams, and myself. In March 1985, I became the longest-running producer of the show, and I was delighted to be invited to reminisce in writing about the show I love: to examine the performances, and personalities of the six individuals listed above. For that is what they are – individuals; each brought their individuality to the rôle of the Doctor, as Andrew Skilleter's excellent portraits of each of the actors as the Doctor demonstrate.

A trip through one's memories brings some pain, and some joy. I'm delighted my trip is dominated by joy. Come with me through the Tardis doors and meet William, Patrick, Jon, Tom, Peter, and Colin. A list of friends or enemies? Undoubtedly, a list of friends.

John Nathan-Turner

·WILLIAM HARTNELL·

In the Beginning

I feel I should be honest from the start by telling you that not only didn't I work with William Hartnell, but, sadly, I never even met him. However, over the five years I have spent as the producer of the longest-running science-fiction series in the world, I did have the pleasure of meeting Heather Hartnell, William's widow, his daughter, Anne, and granddaughter, Judith – not forgetting, Terry Carney, William's son-in-law and former agent. Terry, incidentally, is also the agent of Nicola Bryant, who is the sixth Doctor's current companion, so I'm in regular communication with him.

From meeting William's relatives, I have built up a picture of the man who secured the ongoing success of *Doctor Who*. This picture, combined with my impressions as a viewer of "Bill's" Doctor, makes me feel as though I had been around on the set during those early years. Bill's fierce professionalism, his lack of toleration of fools or amateurs, and his slightly self-opinionated air certainly made him a force to be reckoned with. But his application to the job at hand, and his ferocious dedication to this particular program, set a standard for all actors who have subsequently played the part.

The Character

In a way, the character of the Doctor, as brought to life by Bill, was more than something of an anti-hero. Although a dominant sense of right and justice – forever anxious to thwart evil – prevailed, there was an aggressive irascibility which dominated the portrayal; an impatience, too, of the relatively simple minds of his earth companions.

Doctor Who was originally conceived as only a thirteen-part series. However, right at the beginning, from the moment Verity Lambert, the first producer, convinced Bill to play the part, he had high hopes for the show. He predicted that the show would run for five years at least. What a delight it is to say, how wrong he was! Yet, how right he was in predicting the series' long-term potential.

Verity Lambert was originally asked to aim the show at an audience of nine- to fourteen-year olds, but she quite rightly anticipated that the appeal of the show would not be bound by any age barriers, and she briefed her writers and directors accordingly. It is because of this initial aiming for a "no-age barred" family audience, combined with the fact that the show has always been made by the Drama Serials Department, that I am constantly amazed that anyone would consider the show a children's program. Children's programs are made by the Children's Department. It's as simple as that. Recent audience research reveals that today less than thirty-five to forty percent of our audience is under sixteen. I have reason to believe that from Bill's first appearance, only about fifty percent of the audience were children. A family audience was achieved from the start.

An Unearthly Child

My favorite story of the classic Hartnell years is *An Unearthly Child*, the first-ever story – not just for nostalgia's sake either. Episode one is a remarkable piece of TV drama and, unlike much of the drama made at that time, stands up as excellent science-fiction even today, and William Hartnell's grumpy old Doctor is a delight to behold. His performance captured our imaginations and hearts from the start. I salute you, sir, and I only wish we could have met.

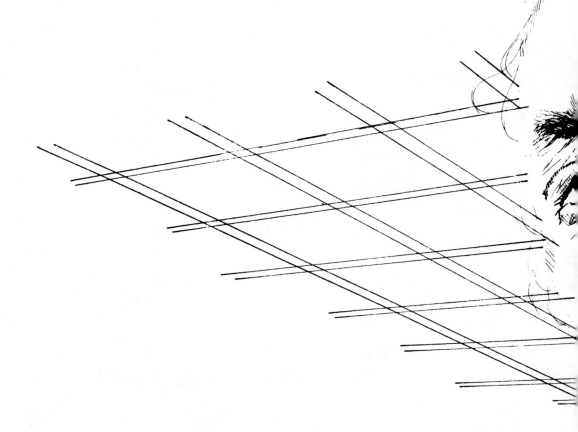

First Meeting

I first met Patrick Troughton in 1969. I had joined BBC TV as a floor assistant, the most junior member of a TV production team, in December of the previous year. One of the very first programs I was allocated to was *Doctor Who*. The job of floor assistant on a show such as *Doctor Who* involves attending one rehearsal in order to get to know the rest of the production team, the script and, of course, the actors. When the show transfers to one of the BBC studios the floor assistant is responsible for ensuring the right actors are on the right set at the right time. In addition, the floor assistant generally "assists" the floor manager or production manager throughout the studio session.

When I attended my first *Doctor Who* rehearsal over in a dingy West London church hall, Patrick and the Doctor's companions, Jamie (Frazer Hines) and Zoe (Wendy Padbury), made me instantly welcome. I remember distinctly the atmosphere of hard work combined with tremendous fun which prevailed in that rehearsal room – a combination I try to encourage now that I am the producer.

First to Fourth

In those days *Doctor Who* was recorded at the Lime Grove Studios in Shepherd's Bush – a rabbit warren of a building, which now houses current affairs programs and Breakfast TV. The main problem with the "Grove" was, and still is, that the dressing rooms are situated on the ground and basement floors and the studios are on the first and fourth floors. And you've probably guessed where *Doctor Who* was recorded – that's right, the fourth floor. So to collect artists for the studio meant a trip down five, or at best four flights of stairs. There was one elevator but, as it was the only elevator in the building, it was never free when you needed it. Add to this horrendous situation, the fact that a typical *Doctor Who* episode is comprised of many short scenes, and the result was a near-neurotic, perspiring, weight-losing floor assistant. I should add that this is the only unpleasant memory I have of my first experience of the show that has become a huge slice of my life.

Patrick – The Actor

Patrick is one of those fine actors who hardly ever stops working. I used to see him regularly at various BBC rehearsal rooms – I worked with him again, by the way, on the excellent *Six Wives of Henry VIII* – and when the BBC acquired what we call the Acton Hilton (a huge purpose-built rehearsal block in North Acton), I saw him even more regularly. We worked together again in the late 1970s on *All Creatures Great and Small*.

In 1982 I proposed to the controller of BBC1 the idea of a ninety-minute special *Doctor Who* program to celebrate the show's twentieth anniversary, entitled *The Five Doctors*. The idea was accepted. After I had obtained the *initial* interest for the project from the four living Doctors: Patrick, Jon, Tom and Peter: I started to investigate when in 1983 it would be best to make the program, and still be able to transmit it in November of that year. The first consideration is the length of the day in terms of daylight. The more hours of daylight to shoot in, equals the more minutes of film shot per day. So I decided June or July would give my unit very long shooting days combined with, hopefully, good weather.

I was about to start engaging the actors when I discovered that Patrick was unable to commit himself during the period, as a project he was doing for an independent company had included an option on his services for a further series. I could have gone ahead with booking the other actors, and hoped that in due course the project for ITV would not be successful and Patrick's option wouldn't be taken up. However, I rang Patrick and asked his feelings about the success or otherwise of the project. Patrick said he thought the project would turn out to be successful. He was right. The show was *Foxy Lady*. Consequently, I moved the shoot for *The Five Doctors* to March 1983. A bad time of the year for hours of daylight and for weather, but I had little choice.

Shooting *The Five Doctors*

Whilst we were filming *The Five Doctors*, in North Wales, we stayed in a small village called Maenturog. There was one hotel where some of the unit stayed (it wasn't big enough for everyone), and a friendly pub where the remainder resided. Most of the leading actors, Doctors and companions, and the production team stayed at the hotel. It was comfortable and pleasant enough, but rather quiet. After a long day's shoot, everyone wants to relax and let their hair down and this hotel wasn't quite the right place to do so. Usually, on our return from shooting everyone would shower and change and then congregate in the hotel bar. As with any film shoot in a quiet area word goes round very quickly that "stars" are in the village.

This shoot was no exception and after a couple of days, we would congregate in the hotel bar to discover it was packed with people wanting autographs, etc. Signing autographs and chatting to the public is part of the "show business" job and the hotel owner was thrilled at the upsurge in business at a bad time of year for tourists. However, one evening Peter Moffatt, the director, and I thought we would visit the other actors and remainder of the team at their pub – we heard they had live music in the bar and the unit was being made extremely welcome. So we gathered together the *Doctor Who* cast from the hotel, and set off on the half-mile walk. As we walked down the hill, I turned round to see that the hotel bar had emptied and the general public was coming with us. The hotel owners were furious! We had taken everyone from the bar. This happened regularly during the shoot, but eventually the owners seemed happy as long as we spent some time in their bar before going elsewhere.

Longleat

It was round about this time that the BBC Enterprises' *Doctor Who* celebration at Longleat was being planned. I had been asked by the Enterprises team to encourage all the leading players to attend. I had been warned, however, by fans and actors alike, that Patrick wouldn't participate. So imagine my surprise when he instantly said "yes."

However, a few days later, Patrick's agent called me to say Pat had now decided not to do it. This is when my persuasive charm went into top gear. I told Pat how important it was to me and he kept putting obstacles in the way – I agreed to everything. Exasperated, he said, "What can I talk about – I was the Doctor so long ago I can't remember much." I explained that the fans of the show would jog his memory and that his presence there would mean everything to them and me. He agreed. I remember though a discussion about personal appearances between Jon (Pertwee), Pat, and I in Wales during filming, when Pat voiced his enormous reservations about appearing as himself in public. Jon stood up and said, "Then why are you doing Longleat?" Pat grimaced and pointed at me. We all laughed loudly – except Pat.

However, Patrick thoroughly enjoyed Longleat. Since then he has decided he liked meeting the fans, and has appeared at the National Film Theatre *Doctor Who* weekend, and at the two mammoth American Conventions in Chicago.

Space Pirates

This story was my first encounter face to face with the Doctor, so it probably isn't surprising that it is my favorite of the Troughton era. It was also written by my favorite *Doctor Who* writer, Robert Holmes. I'm not suggesting that this is the best example of the second Doctor's reign – the story, for me, just has so much nostalgia attached to it.

·JON PERTWEE·

Jon's Doctor Who

As a floor assistant, I worked on two stories in which Jon played the Doctor in the early 1970's – *Colony in Space* and *Ambassadors of Death*. I remember vividly attending an outside rehearsal of one of the stories in a dingy church hall in West London. The director, Michael Ferguson, allowed the cast to do one final run-through of the recording with no holds barred. The cast really enjoyed this. They played each scene with different accents, comic walks, funny noses, etc. It was great fun to watch and, of course, Jon reigned supreme with his amazing array of characters and voices. This ability was very much in evidence in his world-famous radio series *The Navy Lark*. The whole thing was hysterical to watch. A run-through of this kind is often used by directors to help the actors relax, and get all of the laughs out of everyone's system before the serious business of studio recording. Jon was a wonderful leading man; he knew everyone's name – cameramen, sound technicians, everyone – and as I'm sure you can appreciate, this helped to create an excellent atmosphere on the set.

Jon's era as the Doctor from 1970 to 1974, mainly set on earth, was a hugely successful one. Jon did much to promote the series under the guidance of the producer, Barry Letts. Some fans are critical of this era being dominated by earth-bound stories and the regular appearance of U.N.I.T. Although I must confess the familiarity of the earth surroundings on a regular basis did not appeal to me at the time, its success must be acknowledged. One of the reasons the show has remained popular throughout its run is because it has progressed. The U.N.I.T. era was part of that progression, and part and parcel of its appeal to 110 million viewers in fifty-four countries.

Jon the Entertainer

It was many years later that I met Jon again – *Doctor Who* had become a cult in America and the stars of the show and I were traveling regularly to the USA to appear at conventions. Jon is an excellent convention guest – he is a superb

raconteur and is able to relate many amusing incidents from his time as the Doctor. Apart from conventions, the next time I worked with Jon again was on the twentieth anniversary special. Jon agreed immediately to appear in the show, and I was delighted. I had hoped to pair Doctor number three with Jo Grant (Katy Manning) in the program but, when Tom Baker decided not to take part, I decided that Elisabeth (Lis) Sladen (Sarah Jane), should appear as the companion. Jon and Lis got on tremendously well, just as they had when they were in the series together and when they toured America in 1982, promoting the program.

Jon, of all the Doctors, is certainly the most widely experienced: radio, TV, cabaret, pantomime, music hall, variety, etc. If you ever get the opportunity to see Jon in cabaret, don't miss it. I have seen his cabaret act many times, but I never tire of Jon's timing and professionalism. I have been honored on several occasions to act briefly as Jon's "feed" in cabaret, an experience I shall always treasure.

Making the Programs

One is asked regularly at conventions and interviews to recount amusing incidents that occur during the making of *Doctor Who*, and it is always difficult to remember them. Another problem is that something that made a whole film unit collapse into fits of laughter at filming in Tunbridge Wells may seem totally *un*amusing to anyone who wasn't present. In November of 1984 I was appearing at a convention in San José, California, with Jon, and one evening Jon, his lovely wife, Ingeborg, and I went to dinner. Jon reminded me at the dinner of an incident in *The Five Doctors*, which I had temporarily forgotten. There was a film sequence in the show where Jon rescued Sarah Jane, who had fallen down a ravine. After the rescue, the Doctor and Sarah had a conversation in static positions. The weather was icy cold and everyone's breath hung on the air. After rehearsing several times we were ready to go for a take on the dialogue section, when the cameraman noticed that despite the make-up, Jon and Lis had turned blue in the face with cold. The only answer to the problem was for the two actors to smack each other hard in the face to put some color back into their complexions. Watching Jon and Lis hit each other, while giggling, was very funny. I offered to help, but the offer was refused!

I have many nicknames at the BBC – many of them unsuitable to print here! The most commonly used is J.N.T. (or TNT, whenever I'm explosive). Jon always calls me J, which just goes to prove even an abbreviation can be abbreviated.

I know Jon still retains enormous fondness for *Doctor Who*, and I feel sure he would return to the show to play the Doctor any time he was asked.

The Daemons

Not only is this my favorite story of the third Doctor, it is Jon Pertwee's as well. Moreover, it is the story most fondly remembered by Nicholas Courtney (the Brigadier). Recently on a trip to the USA, I was staying in Illinois, and *The Daemons* was playing nightly on the local PBS channel, so I had another chance to view the

story. Black magic stories definitely have a place in the world of *Doctor Who*, and this is where *The Daemons* excels. With a masterful story, the late, great, Roger Delgado in fine form, Jon's Doctor at his most "Doctorish" (there is an excellent confrontation between the Doctor and a British publican in episode one), and some excellent visual effects, it is a clear winner. Added to this there is a large proportion of location work, based in a delightful rural English village. The ingredients combine to make this, in my opinion, one of the best-ever *Doctor Who* tales.

· TOM BAKER ·

The Talons of Weng-Chiang

I was introduced to Tom Baker during the studio recording sessions of *The Talons of Weng-Chiang*. *Talons* was the last story of the 1976–77 season of *Doctor Who* and outgoing producer Philip Hinchcliffe had invited incoming producer Graham Williams and myself to attend the recording. I had just been given an attachment (a 12-month trial period in a new job) as production unit manager, and my first assignment was with *Doctor Who*. I was taking over from erstwhile P.U.M., Christopher D'Oyly-John, who had been looking after the show's finances and logistics for three years. I had been assigned to other productions in the BBC and this was a return to *Doctor Who* after a five-year absence. I remember being fairly apprehensive about the whole thing; taking over *the* most complex production that the BBC makes in terms of overall organization was a daunting prospect. However, Christopher had instigated a very thorough hand-over and it was certainly entertaining for me to watch *Doctor Who* "in recording" from the gallery for the first time. The gallery is one level above the studio floor, and it is there that the producer, director, vision mixer, lighting director, sound supervisor, etc. sit watching the studio's output with the various heads of department issuing their instructions to their assistants in order to achieve what the director and producer require.

Visual Effects

I remember that the first visual effect I watched from this elevated position was supposed to be a table collapsing. I'm afraid I can't remember now why it had to collapse, but I do recall it was important to the story. After an interminable wait for the VISFX (Visual Effects) crew to rig the table, everyone was ready to tape the sequence. The machines moved into the record mode; the red lights outside the studio were flashing and the cue was given for the effect to take place. Twenty seconds passed with tension mounting in the gallery. Eventually, there was a minute fizz and a small section of the leg of the table fell to the ground. Everyone, including

myself, laughed long and hard, but then I realized the tremendous pressure of time in the *Doctor Who* studio. Although the director, David Maloney, laughed as well, it was brief, and he instructed everyone to set up the effect again as quickly as possible, as there were still so many scenes left to do. I looked at the recording order, and what seemed like an impossible task lay in front of everyone. Nevertheless, thanks to David's expertise and that of the rest of the team, the breakneck speed recording achieved its goal. Everything was "in the can" with only a short overrun beyond ten o'clock. "Is it always like this?" I said to Chris D'Oyly-John. "Always!" he replied. "Welcome back to *Doctor Who*."

Production Unit Manager to Producer

My three years as Graham Williams' production unit manager passed very rapidly. We recorded one show in the Pebble Mill Studio – this was the first time a *Doctor Who* production had been made inside a BBC regional studio.

I must admit, it felt very strange working on *Doctor Who* in Birmingham. *Doctor Who* was so firmly established in London that we all felt slightly lost. However, Tom breezed into the studios, greeted everyone as though we were part of the London crew, and although the recording suffered from a number of technical breakdowns (not surprising with brand-new equipment), the production was completed and "the townies" set off for London again at the end, heading for our proper home.

After my first two years as P.U.M., Graham asked me if I would like to become his associate producer. I was really excited at the prospect, but due to union agreements and problems of billing, the offer never came to fruition. I had always wanted to become a producer, ever since I joined BBC TV, and I was bitterly disappointed at being so near, yet so far.

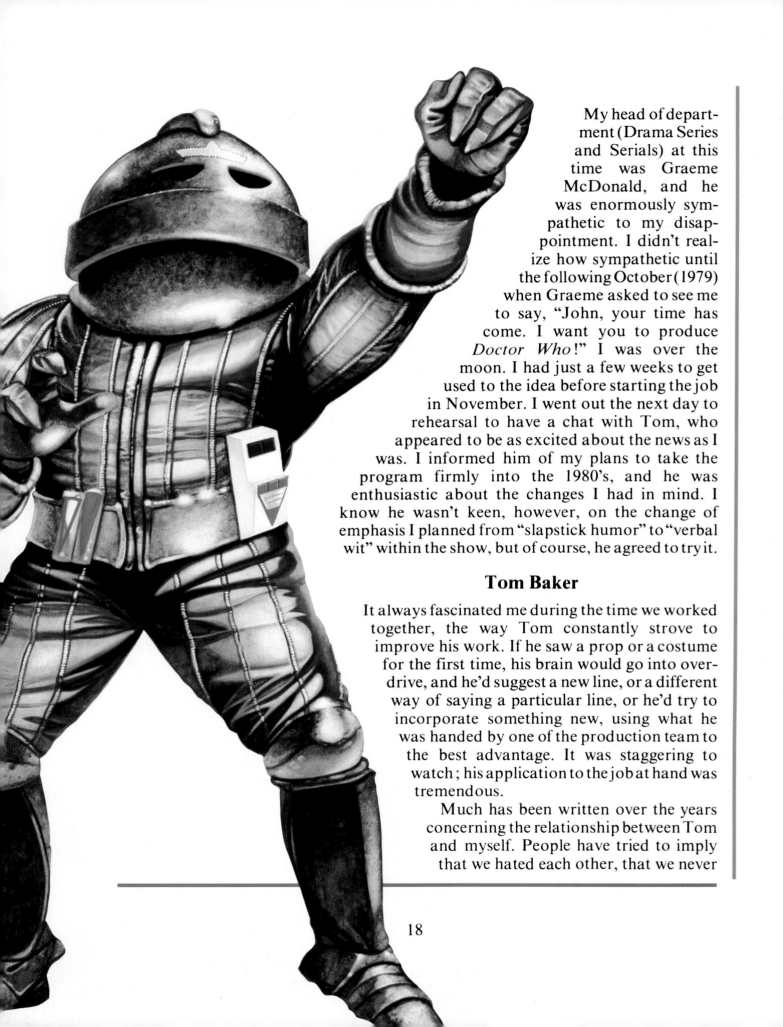

My head of department (Drama Series and Serials) at this time was Graeme McDonald, and he was enormously sympathetic to my disappointment. I didn't realize how sympathetic until the following October (1979) when Graeme asked to see me to say, "John, your time has come. I want you to produce *Doctor Who*!" I was over the moon. I had just a few weeks to get used to the idea before starting the job in November. I went out the next day to rehearsal to have a chat with Tom, who appeared to be as excited about the news as I was. I informed him of my plans to take the program firmly into the 1980's, and he was enthusiastic about the changes I had in mind. I know he wasn't keen, however, on the change of emphasis I planned from "slapstick humor" to "verbal wit" within the show, but of course, he agreed to try it.

Tom Baker

It always fascinated me during the time we worked together, the way Tom constantly strove to improve his work. If he saw a prop or a costume for the first time, his brain would go into overdrive, and he'd suggest a new line, or a different way of saying a particular line, or he'd try to incorporate something new, using what he was handed by one of the production team to the best advantage. It was staggering to watch; his application to the job at hand was tremendous.

Much has been written over the years concerning the relationship between Tom and myself. People have tried to imply that we hated each other, that we never

18

spoke directly to each other, and that generally the last Tom Baker season of *Doctor Who* was produced in a thoroughly miserable atmosphere. This is simply not true.

Let it be said, once and for all, that Tom and I had a good working relationship. The chemistry between the producer and leading actor in this particular program is tremendously important. *Doctor Who* as a commodity does not cease vis-à-vis these two individuals at ten p.m. on studio nights. There is a tremendous amount of activity outside the walls of the BBC which takes place to the benefit of the show. Personal appearances, charity work, exhibitions, merchandise approval, press receptions, talk shows, etc. are all part and parcel of the commodity at hand. I seriously think it would be impossible to undertake all this peripheral activity if producer and star didn't get on. And, if anyone is still in doubt, apart from the list of work inside and outside the BBC, Tom and I spent time together socially.

During my first year as a producer, Tom became very ill and started to lose weight rapidly. This was of great concern to Tom, but he wouldn't see a doctor. As I'm sure you know, for each four-part story there are two studio recording sessions with a fortnight in between. During these sessions we record all the scenes in the sets that are erected. This is called multi-episodic recording and usually means we record the end of the story first. In fact, it is only at the initial read-through that the story is heard as a whole play, until editing takes place. Tom's illness took place during the making of the story *State of Decay*, and if you look at the finished product you can tell which scenes with Tom were recorded in which sessions, as his weight loss was so dramatic. Also, combined with his illness, his naturally curly hair went straight. The make-up department set Tom's hair in carmen rollers for the

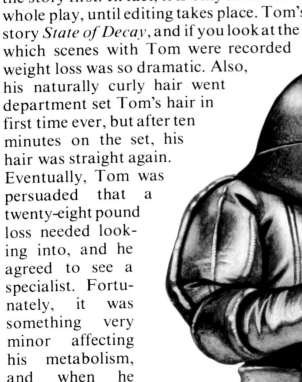

first time ever, but after ten minutes on the set, his hair was straight again. Eventually, Tom was persuaded that a twenty-eight pound loss needed look-ing into, and he agreed to see a specialist. Fortu-nately, it was something very minor affecting his metabolism, and when he found out it was

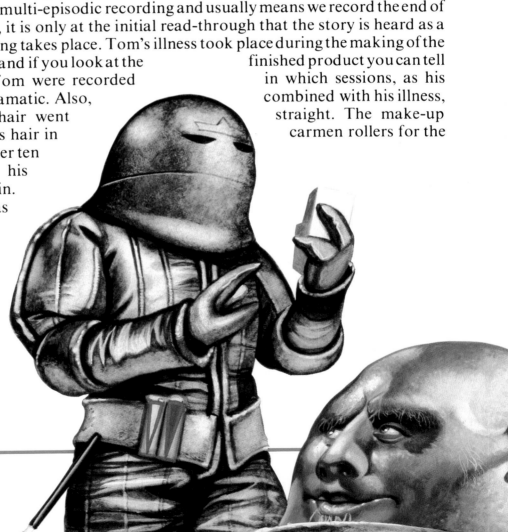

less serious than he feared, his weight started to re-stabilize quite quickly.

Tom's Resignation

It was round about this time in 1980 that Tom decided to relinquish the role of the Doctor. His decision came as something of a shock – Tom's seven years were a major landmark in the program's existence. However, I respected his decision and we agreed to withhold any announcement of his intentions to leave until he, and the show, could benefit most from the news. However, we were not able to time the announcement of his departure as we had hoped.

Tom Baker was the first and only person to have two likenesses in the Madame Tussaud's Waxworks Museum in London. One was commissioned just after I took over the show; the other was a cactus-covered replica (Meglos) used as part of *The Doctor Who Experience*, a separate attraction at the Waxworks, featuring many favorite monsters from the show. Juliet Simkins, the public relations officer at Tussaud's, suggested we organize a photocall of Tom and the two waxwork images of him. I agreed, and one wet weekday morning the national press turned up in force outside Tussaud's in the Marylebone Road. After the photos were taken and the photographers had gone back to Fleet Street, Tom and I went to the pub opposite for a drink. We hadn't been there very long when the barman said there was a call for me. It was my secretary. She told me that there had been a leak to the *Daily Mirror* that Tom was leaving, and a news reporter and photographer were on their way to Tussaud's to track us down. Tom and I rapidly finished our drinks, jumped into a taxi, and went to another bar in the West End. From there I made several phone calls, and called a press conference at the BBC's Cavendish Place premises, and we then lay low for an hour or two.

The press conference was scheduled for two p.m. and as we were journeying to the venue by taxi, Tom turned to me and suggested we have some fun at the conference ("departure" conferences are fairly somber affairs) and implied that the next Doctor could well be a woman. I agreed.

When we arrived at 10A Cavendish Place, the place was packed – TV news teams, reporters, photographers, radio interviewers, etc. As we tried to fight our way through to the front of the barrage of bustling newsmen, one reporter, not recognizing us, suggested we take our turn! We finally got to the front, Tom announced his departure and his reasons for leaving, and ended thus: "I wish the new *Doctor Who* the very best of luck, whoever he or she is!" The crowd chorused, "She?" "Did you say *she*?" At which point Tom said, "I've probably said too much already – ask the producer, John Nathan-Turner," and with that, he departed into the garden to pose for photographers. I was left holding the baby, facing an array of hopeful faces. I explained that as far as I was concerned, it was feasible to have a female Doctor, but no firm decision had been taken. It was seven o'clock that evening before Tom and I finished. All the radio shows were done, photos taken, interviews live by phone to America, and Tom ended the day live on *Nationwide* with the Tardis.

The following day the front pages of many national newspapers had been given over to the news. The conference had been a huge success.

At three a.m. the morning after the press call, I was woken up by the telephone. It was an Australian radio station, Radio 2ZW from Sydney. "Hello, Mr. Nathan-Turner, this is Radio 2ZW from Sydney calling you *live* – we understand that Tom Baker is leaving *Doctor Who*. Could we discuss it, please?" "But it's three a.m.," I croaked. "Not over here, it isn't!" was the reply.

Such was the shock that Tom was leaving, that the whole world seemed interested.

Tom and Lalla

A few months later there was to be another *Doctor Who* press sensation. Tom and Lalla Ward had been seeing each other "off the set" as well as on for about a year. They seemed to have an on/off relationship, and no one was ever really sure during this time when it was "on" and when it was "off." Believing people's private lives are very much just that – private – I never really stopped to think of Tom and Lalla as a couple. Others did, but I refused to join in with their speculation.

One morning Tom rang me in the office to tell me that he and Lalla were to be married. I must admit I was very surprised. Lalla, by now, had left the program and she made an official announcement of their intentions through the BBC press office. Immediately, phones were jammed with newspapers wanting a posed photograph of the happy couple. I advised Tom and Lalla to let me call a conference and get it over with. However, they were adamant – no photocall; no press conference. When, two hours later, the press besieged Lalla's flat and the BBC rehearsal block, they changed their minds. Once again, Tom was in the news (and on the news), this time with a much more pleasant announcement.

Afterwards

Tom's last story as the Doctor was called *Logopolis* and this story ended with the traditional regeneration – Tom's face blending into the features of the new Doctor – Peter Davison. It was an emotional scene to shoot –

Tom's last line, "This is the end – but the moment has been prepared for," having a double poignancy.

I remember that after the final scene involving Tom had been recorded, Tom slipped away from TV Centre without a word, disappearing into the night – no farewells, no goodbyes – a solitary figure heading for a new life. And what an exciting life it was – Tom's first job after *Doctor Who* was as Oscar Wilde in *Feasting with Panthers* at the Chichester Festival Theatre; then he played Long John Silver in *Treasure Island* at the Mermaid Theatre, London. I went to see both productions, and met up with Tom afterwards. Shortly after this, he appeared as Sherlock Holmes in *The Hound of the Baskervilles* for BBC TV producer Barry Letts. Tom was back at the Acton Rehearsal Rooms again, in great form and with no regrets.

It must have been soon after this that I first sounded out Tom about *The Five Doctors*, a tribute to *Doctor Who*'s twenty-year run. He seemed initially keen and wanted to see a script. The script for this show did give Eric Saward, my script editor, and myself a number of headaches, but eventually in December 1982 we had the first seventy pages.

I was filming *The King's Demons* that December at Bodiham Castle, an hour and a half's drive from Brighton, where I have a weekend apartment. Tom was touring with the Royal Shakespeare Company in *Educating Rita* and happened to be on at the Theatre Royal, Brighton.

I left location one day, journeyed to Brighton, where I changed out of my thermal underwear and Wellington boots, and went to see

Educating Rita, having arranged to meet Tom at his hotel afterwards. It was a thoroughly enjoyable evening. Tom was, on the whole, happy with the script; he agreed to take part in the special and we stayed drinking in the hotel until three a.m.

Imagine my surprise and disappointment when shortly afterwards, Jean Diamond, Tom's agent and close friend, called to tell me he didn't wish to take part. I couldn't believe it. I was doubly surprised as Tom had arranged to join me for lunch the following day. Jean thought this odd too, and promised to call me back. When she phoned, she explained that Tom was very sorry, but he didn't wish to take part in the special, as he didn't wish to be "one of the five," and in any case he'd left *Doctor Who* behind now. She added that, under the circumstances, he wouldn't be coming to lunch the following day.

The next day an extremely charming letter arrived from Tom, which I shall always treasure. However, I had a problem. How could I do a story called *The Five Doctors* without Tom? I was recasting the late William Hartnell's Doctor anyway – two re-casts would be silly. I did have in the archives the footage of the story *Shada*, which was never completed, and consequently, never shown. I rang Tom to have one last go at persuading him to change his mind. However, he was still adamant. I asked if I could use clips from *Shada*, so that he could still appear briefly in the special, and he agreed. I rang Lalla too (by this time, they were living separately), and she also agreed. The special was saved.

I should explain at this point that if a repeat of a show is planned, no permission from the actors is needed, but if segments of a show are to be used in another production, permission must be sought.

In March and April 1983, we filmed and recorded *The Five Doctors*. I had arranged yet another major press call to announce the project, the highlight of which was to be a picture of Tom, Jon, Peter, Patrick and Richard Hurndall (the recast of the first Doctor). I had asked Tom, through his agent Jean, if he would turn up for this, as he would be appearing in the end product. I always had a feeling at the back of my head that Tom wouldn't turn up, especially after hearing Tom's feelings about *Doctor Who* from Jean. So, I arranged to borrow Tom's waxwork from Madame Tussaud's, just in case. As I suspected, Tom didn't arrive. So, when the estate car carrying Tom's prostrate form arrived, we set it up on location with the other real actors, and much to the amusement of the press, got our five Doctor's photograph, and the special project was launched.

I still see Tom from time to time – the last time being in November 1983 in Chicago, and I know his fondness for the show will never wane. Similarly, my fondness for him will never wane.

Keeper of Traken

This is my favorite story from Tom's era. Not only is it a marvelous story, but John Black's "organic" conception and visual style, complemented by the wonderful costumes of Amy Roberts, made the show a feast for the eyes. Johnny Byrne's script, reintroducing the Master, includes eloquent dialogue, and Tom is in fine form, particularly when performing with Anthony Ainley.

Who Could Ever Replace Tom Baker?

When Tom Baker decided to relinquish the role of *Doctor Who* I was faced with a tremendous problem. Tom had played the part for a mammoth seven years – the longest in the show's history. How could I replace him? Should I look for a Doctor who was as eccentric as Tom, or should I try something completely different? Should I cast an unknown? For several weeks, I constantly pondered these questions. Coming to no firm conclusion, I finally decided to approach the problem from a different angle.

What did I want in a new Doctor? I decided to make a list of requirements.

1. Heroism – the Doctor must be heroic.
2. Youthfulness – I wanted a younger Doctor for a more youthful audience.
3. Vulnerability – we needed a Doctor who could get it wrong occasionally. This is something the series hadn't had with Tom.

At this point, I began to see that the task wasn't impossible, and my excitement mounted. Fitting together the pieces of a puzzle like this is one of the real pleasures of being a producer.

4. Straight hair – Tom's curly locks had become so famous. We needed an opposite image.

Peter Davison

The first time I met Peter Davison was in a conference room at the BBC's Television Centre. Producer Bill Sellars had gathered together the stars and production team of his new project, *All Creatures Great and Small*. At that time, Peter was the least well-known of the actors present, and I remember being struck immediately by his warmth and charm. After watching Peter filming on location in the role of Tristan, I was even more impressed by his sensitivity and honesty as an actor. Within a few months, the British television viewing public – all nineteen million of them – were obviously as impressed as I had been, and Peter achieved overnight success and stardom.

Thus, when I had assessed what I was looking for: a good actor, equally happy in dramatic or comic roles; there is always a place for comic wit in *Doctor Who*; someone with straight hair and an aura of heroism; a vulnerable youth: suddenly, Peter Davison's name sprang to mind. I picked up the telephone – Peter was amazed, but very interested. I knew then I'd found my fifth Doctor.

However, Peter needed time to think. For any actor a series such as *Doctor Who*, while providing a golden opportunity, is restricting and requires total commitment. Peter was also afraid that casting him would be so "against type" that he felt the audience wouldn't accept him as the Doctor. We met for lunch, and on several other occasions over the next two or three weeks. We were also in constant touch by telephone. Television producers are very persuasive individuals. They make the decisions, and they also take the risks. When things don't work out, it is always the producer who takes the blame. Consequently, most of us are adamant about our decisions – if we don't think we've made the right choice, no one else will!

Still, what if I hadn't convinced Peter that my decision was right? What if he'd turned it down in the end? I started to think about other candidates. I picked up *Spotlight*, the actors casting directory – and snapped it shut. I'd wait until I had a final answer from Peter. A few weeks after I'd first approached Peter, a call came from his agent, John Mahoney. Peter would love to play the part!

Although Peter had only fairly recently gained fame, he had been around for some time. He trained at the Central School of Speech and Drama and his first engagement was at the Nottingham Playhouse. After several theater jobs, his television debut came as Tom Holland in *Love for Lydia*, before the role of Tristan beckoned him to the BBC. Three hugely successful series of *All Creatures Great and Small* were followed by hit situation comedy series *Holding the Fort* and *Sink or Swim*.

Choosing the Image

The fifth *Doctor Who* needed a fresh new image. Peter and I had several brainstorming sessions with regard to the fifth Doctor's costume. We discussed everything from collapsible top hats to polo jodhpurs; from striped blazers to shorts. Eventually, we decided on the Victorian cricketer's image which proved so popular, and which we capitalized on in such stories as *Four to Doomsday* and *Frontios*, using cricketing techniques, and in *Black Orchid* we even saw how brilliant the Doctor was at playing the game.

New Time Slot

At the time we were holding our costume discussions the controller of BBC1 decided that *Doctor Who* should relinquish its traditional Saturday early evening slot in favor of a twice-weekly slot. After eighteen years, it was a decision that provoked anger and concern – protests flooded the BBC offices of the controller and the *Doctor Who* office. The *Guardian* newspaper, in an unprecedented step, devoted its leader to the "tragedy" of moving *Doctor Who* from its "traditional as tea and crumpets" transmission day. However, despite the criticism and petitions, the move provided dividends – the viewing figures doubled the previous season's lower ratings. From viewing figures of five and a half million we moved to ten million.

This Is Your Nightmare

It was during the transmission of Peter's first season as the Doctor that he was chosen to be the subject of *This Is Your Life*. Peter's wife, Sandra Dickinson, John Mahoney, his agent, and I were among the very few involved in the project. As you probably know, if the "suspect" hears about the project, it is immediately abandoned. All I had to do was get Peter out of his house as early as possible on the day of the show. Sandra could then go to the camera rehearsals without suspicion, and I would ensure that Peter, John, and I turned up at 4.30 p.m. in Trafalgar Square. Quite easy, I hear you say. It was a nightmare!

To begin with, *This Is Your Life* approached me about three to four months before the event. Mysterious phone calls from Thames TV with regards to clips, the Tardis, Cybermen, etc. flooded in. I had to tell my secretary, Jane Judge, what was going on. She was as thrilled as I was, but the rest of my team became neurotic. They

couldn't understand what was so office door was constantly closed, abrupt changes in conversation mad, including me. Finally, the big secret. My ever-open the whispering, and were driving everyone day came.

I had invited Peter for an early lunch at a nearby restaurant, supposedly to talk about the next season. I must admit that if there is one topic that's banned from conversation it's incredibly hard to avoid it. I kept saying to myself, "We'll talk about anything except *This Is Your Life*" – and every time there was a lull in the conversation, a booming voice in my head was screaming, "*This Is Your Life, This Is Your Life*." Somehow, we stumbled through lunch and returned to the office.

There, one of the "mysterious" calls occurred, telling me that the Tardis was taking ages to move, so there'd be a delay. I'd told Peter that we were doing a series of trailers for ABC TV in Australia, so I sent him off to change into the Doctor's costume.

As we waited for everything to be ready for "the Australian trailers," Peter claimed afterwards that this was the only time his suspicions were aroused. When my staff answer the phones in the office, they say simply "Dr. Who". Peter loved to pick up the phone and say just that, whenever he was visiting, and listen to the usually speechless person on the other end. Of course it was vital that afternoon that he didn't do so, in case it was one of those "mysterious" calls. And he was slightly taken aback when everyone else started diving to pick up the phone from the other side of the room.

Time passed slowly, and conversation became stilted. Finally, a call came through – the chauffeur-driven car had arrived. We had another near-revelation when a friend of my secretary's passed the door and said, "Hello, did you know there's a car downstairs from *This Is*..." Jane did a rugby tackle and pushed her down the corridor.

At Trafalgar Square I got Peter into position outside the Tardis, and gave the "action" signal. Out of the box came Jane Fielding (Tegan), Sarah Sultan (Nyssa), Matthew Waterhouse (Adric), Anthony Ainley (The Master), followed by Eamonn and the famous red book. What they edited out of the show was Peter yelling, "I'll kill him! I'll kill him!" as he realized he'd been had. The intrigue and strain were well worth it!

Bloopers

People often ask me about "bloopers" and the possibility of the BBC issuing a videotape about *Doctor Who* bloopers. Like amusing incidents on the set, they are often only hysterically funny when they happen. However, one involving Peter I still find hilarious.

We were filming *The Awakening* in an English country village. The action called for a horse and cart driven by the Doctor to ride into shot, and stop at the church gate, while the Doctor and company disembarked. At the rehearsals the horse wouldn't get near the gate, and ruined the shot. The gate had been supplied by our designer – it was an elaborate lych-gate, complete with roof, and climbing ivy – all made out of scenery. To help calm our horse, it was decided to place the horse's mare on the other side of the gate, in the church grounds. The cameras rolled, the director yelled, "Action," and the horse and cart rounded the corner. It stopped at the gate, the Doctor jumped down, but the horse spying his mate was no longer afraid of the scenery, and decided to join his mate. The lych-gate was demolished. We all roared with laughter, except the designer! The gate was so badly damaged that we had to use this as the "take" – cutting the falling gate of course.

Cinderella

In Christmas 1982 I was asked to direct a pantomime at the Assembly Theatre in Tunbridge Wells. I had written a pantomime *Cinderella* many years before, which I had directed several times including once at The Theatre Royal, Drury Lane, with a star-studded cast including Sheila Hancock, Peter O'Toole, Judi Dench, Nigel Stock, and Elaine Stritch.

I liked working with Peter so much I decided to ask him and his vivacious wife, Sandra, to star in the show. They agreed; Peter playing Buttons, and Sandra playing Misozel, Cinderella's fairy godmother. As Baron Hard-Up I chose Anthony "The Master" Ainley. I think the highlight of Peter's engaging performance as Buttons was the now-famous belly-dance, which Peter performed in "drag". I remember Peter not being at all keen on putting on "drag," but when he saw how ridiculous the costume was his fears were dispelled.

Peter's Decision

When Peter decided to leave, it was his decision, and his decision alone. I wanted him to do at least another year, but he wanted to concentrate on other things, and he has certainly been busy since he left – TV series, theater, and documentaries. To Peter with whom I worked solidly and happily for nearly seven years, "Cheers, mate!"

The Caves of Androzani

The Caves of Androzani was Peter Davison's last story, and my favorite of the Davison years. The show had a fine production team: the talented direction of Graeme Harper, an excellent cast and, most importantly, the wit and magic of a Robert Holmes script. Peter as the Doctor was in particularly fine form – his characterization of the Doctor at its most complete. The story has all this, plus the added interest of the regeneration, heralding yet another Doctor.

COLIN BAKER

Colin – The Villain

I first met the actor who became the sixth Doctor at the read-through of a story called *Arc of Infinity*. Ron Jones, the director, and I cast Colin as Maxil, the Commander of the Chancellory Guard on the Doctor's home planet, Gallifrey. We both admired Colin's work over the years, and we considered him ideal for this rather sinister role. Because of Colin's huge success in *The Brothers* as Paul Merroney, a forerunner of TV drama's nastiest character, J.R. Ewing, he was regularly cast as the baddie on the box. He even played King Rat in pantomime. The role of Maxil suited him perfectly.

Arc of Infinity had a super cast: Michael Gough, Elspet Gray, Leonard Sachs, Paul Jerricho, etc., and I remember Colin was usually to be found making technicians laugh with his outrageous wit, whenever he wasn't required on set. At the producer's run-through at the North Acton rehearsal rooms, I commented to Ron Jones that Colin's performance was a little too "arch" for my liking and this resulted in Colin being tagged "Archie" by the cast for the remainder of the production.

It was whilst working on *Arc of Infinity* in 1982 that Colin and his charming wife, Marion, became close friends with my assistant floor manager, Lynn Richards (known affectionately as Snow White) and her husband-to-be. Lynn decided to get married in America, and have two receptions: one in the USA, and one in the UK. Twenty or so of the "Who" team were invited to the English reception, and we sat around together in the garden of a large country house, with Colin recounting an endless stream of funny anecdotes, wickedly accurate impressions, and acid comments. I thought at the time how very different Colin was to Peter Davison, and as I was about to ask Peter if he would stay with the program for another (fourth) year, I remember thinking that if Peter decided to leave, I already had a strong contender for the most sought-after part in British TV.

October 1982

It is usually in the October of one year that it needs to be decided if the leading actor

is going to stay for the year after the next year. (I think this indicates how much forward planning has to go into *Doctor Who*.) So in October 1982 I was to ask Peter if he would appear in the 1984/85 season. Peter wanted more time to decide about staying on, so May 1983 became the deadline for a decision on the fifth Doctor's fourth season.

It was some time after the wedding reception that Snow White (Lynn Richards) came to see me to suggest Colin as the next *Doctor Who*. Little did she know that Peter might be leaving, or that Colin was the hot contender. I always maintain that there is no substitute for a good idea, and I was terribly pleased someone else had also considered Colin.

Later in 1982 Colin was touring in a play with Eleanor Summerfield (wife of Leonard Sachs) and Gerald Flood (voice of Kamelion) and the tour took them to the Theatre Royal, Brighton. As I was at my flat that weekend, I decided to meet

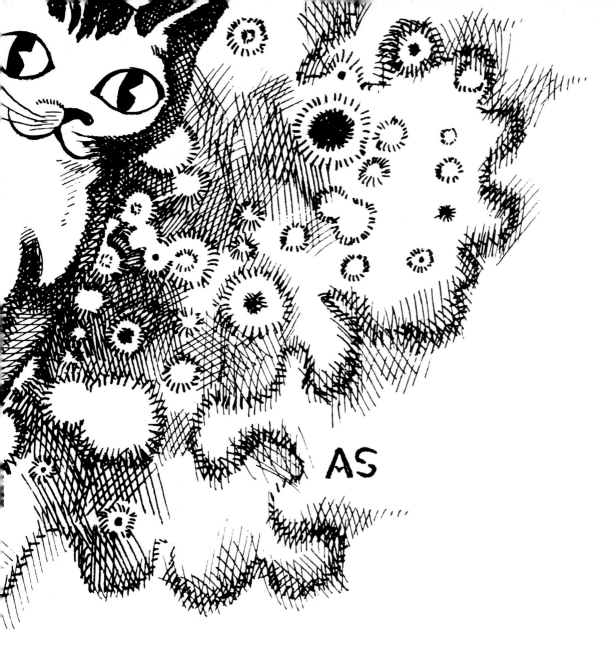

Colin and Gerald and chat over not-so-old times. It was a delightful lunchtime, and by now I was sure Colin would make a perfect Doctor Who. However, for obvious reasons, I mentioned not a thing to Colin; just enjoyed his company and laughed a great deal.

Colin Baker – The Sixth Doctor Who

The following May, Peter decided to leave, so I telephoned Colin and asked him to come and see me. He suspected, because I had contacted him direct, and not via his agent, that the purpose of the meeting was anything but work. In fact, he thought I was going to try to talk him into opening a fête on behalf of the "Who" team. So, when I asked him how he'd feel about taking over *Doctor Who*, his mouth fell open, there was a very long pause, he leaped to his feet and said, "Yes, please!"

There followed a series of meetings over the next few weeks. I gave Colin endless armfuls of old stories as research, and we discussed at length what he felt he could bring of himself to the part. The particular responsibilities of the rôle were discussed too; the conventions, the charity work, the fêtes, the personal appearances, the sheer weight of the post, plus so much peripheral activity. None of this fazed Colin – after all he'd experienced "stardom" of this kind when he was in *The Brothers*. I offered him the part, we shook hands and went out to celebrate.

At the end of one of our discussions, Colin and I went to the Bush Hotel on Shepherd's Bush Green for a drink. The Bush has an upstairs fringe theater and is extremely popular. Imagine our surprise when Peter Davison and Sandra Dickinson arrived to see the play upstairs and found us chatting in a corner. I wanted absolute secrecy about our discussions until negotiations were complete and I was ready to announce the news. Colin and I thought we handled the chance meeting quite brilliantly. Colin said he'd dropped in to buy some video equipment at a bargain store on the Green, and Peter seemed not to suspect a thing. The following day at the rehearsal, Peter said he knew who the next Doctor Who was going to be.

"Who?" I enquired innocently.

"Colin Baker, of course," he replied.

"What on earth gives you that idea?" I said.

"You hate the Bush Hotel, and never go there, so you were obviously in conference where you thought no one would see you!"

Oh well. I swore Peter to secrecy, but it just proves a producer can't go anywhere with someone without another person knowing what you're up to.

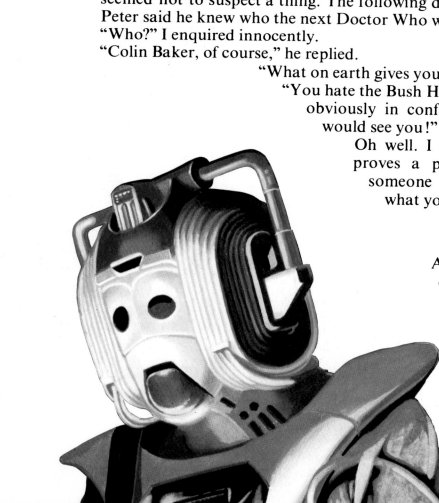

Colin's Costume

After a highly successful press conference announcing Colin as the new Doctor, the inevitable subject of costume turned up. An excellent costume designer,

Pat Godfrey, was engaged and after endless discussions, I suggested a "totally tasteless" costume using clashing colors, checks, patterns, and so on. BBC costume designers are highly skilled and highly trained, but not in designing "totally tasteless" clothes. Pat did many different designs, which she thought hideously tasteless, but we thought fairly *tasteful*. In the end, Pat designed the costume as seen, with many small panels, etc., and Colin and I picked the colors and patterns to fill in the gaps. I think everyone agrees as far as our intention to achieve costume that is garish and without taste, we succeeded, though Colin now has a great liking for its boldness. This appeal is echoed in his many fan letters!

As you read this book, Colin will have completed a whole season, plus one story (*The Twin Dilemma*). The 1984/5 season is, in my opinion, a tour de force for Colin. He has placed his mark indelibly on the rôle in a very short space of time. He has seized the part by the scruff of its neck and made it, for the time being, his own, adding his own brand of humor and eccentricity.

Vengeance on Varos

To select a favorite story of mine to demonstrate Colin's Doctor is quite difficult, due to lack of choice. (At the time of writing, Colin has only completed seven stories). Nevertheless, a choice must be made and so let it be *Vengeance on Varos*, an excellently bizarre story by Philip Martin, featuring a superb monster, Sil, and some extremely witty dialogue. Here's to Colin's appearance in many such stories as this!

PRINTED IN BELGIUM BY

proost

INTERNATIONAL BOOK PRODUCTION